In the Absence of Sons

In the Absence of Sons

A Chapbook of Poems by

Carol Lipszyc

Cover design by Shay Culligan
Cover photography by Yatharth roy vibhakar
https://unsplash.com/@yatharthroyvibhakar

Photograph of Carol Lipszyc at Lake Champlain
by Michael Carrino

ISBN: 978-1-952326-32-5

Kelsay Books
502 South 1040 East, A-119
American Fork, Utah, 84003

Acknowledgments

The Ekphrastic Review: "Straight Back Chair"

The Heart is Improvisational An Anthology in Poetic Form:
 "Slumbering Woman" and "Buoy"

Frontiers, A Journal of Women Studies: "Slumbering Woman"

Per Contra: "Buoy"

the lonely crowd@the lonely press and *the lonely crowd/spring/new
 home of the short story:* "Short Ode to Summer."

Canadian Woman Studies. Women Writing 4: Remembering:
 "Letter for Emily D."

The Eloquent Atheist Positive Atheism with Humanist Nuances:
 "Fear of Science."

Room: "In Mild Praise of Fractions."

Thank you to Michael Carrino and Kenneth Sherman
for their reading and recommendations.

Contents

In Mild Praise of Fractions

Spool of odd and even numbers knot
tightly around my fingers.
Fractions like hieroglyphs
people the tethered pages
of my grade school days.

At the hub of our long-winded kitchen,
turquoise table on a checkerboard
floor. Mother slices red apples on a pine wood
board: "How many quarters,"
she quizzes, "make up one apple?"

I stare blankly till the apple browns,
its juice runs dry.

"Four," baby sister chimes,
moon on her left,
sun on her right.
"Each slice is one-quarter."

What did I know or care of fractions?
I befriended a half-sister and brother
from a family divided;
lost one mitten out of two in a deep drift of snow;
had two canine teeth out of four
pulled to fit my small, pert mouth.

I'd grown suspicious of fractions—
their power to contract.

But Mother and Sister Linda
saw with the Eyes of Horus,
the golden God of Mathematics
who blessed all parts of the whole
their irises, blue rings of light, radiating
equivalence.

House of Mirrors

I remember a woman lovely
as memory acts out its treason,
who built a house of mirrors
in the prime of her girlhood season.

How many fast admired
the image she revived
of beauty seemingly preserved
of beauty rarified.

She saved her trove of copper praise
like coins she could amass,
this age-defiant Alice
captured in her looking glass.

She primped and pranced as if on cue
for love's facsimile
and dabbled in the guise of art
with specious vanity.

To read a script by her own hand,
its pages cut from youth,
while chance suspended on a string
the fame she long pursued.

Dental Examination at Angelina's Restaurant

They set a date in mid-town Toronto,
dispensing profile pics, bios
from a vending machine of love.

At the scene: cherry lip stain on wineglass
spiral loops of pasta in white ceramic bowls.
Above them, crystal beads cast as retail stars,
brass lobe mounted on a blue bell ceiling
of tile and foam.

"How comfortable does this feel,"
he asks, lightly fingering her mouth.
Reclining, she succumbs to his eyes,
the scales on his fingers, the upturned curl
at the corner of his mouth.

His appetite grows—soon he wants more:
x-rays, impressions, reasons—reasons why,
incidents, facts, blood.
His silver-bellied blade
angled on soft, epithelial tissue,
he makes a small incision.
"Let's have a good look," he probes.

Feet tingling, fingers pressed on padded armchair,
she expels a confession on a satin-band napkin,
the imprint of her words, inscrutable.

Nonplussed, he praises the meal,
the atmosphere of the place, her company.

She pares down her words
into mineral and marrow,

driving the night's syntax
to a full stop.

Interrogator and interrogated
preserving some small monopoly

one
over
the
other.

Slumbering Woman

See this woman who dons injury
like a vintage mink stole,
weathered tail wrapped
around her shoulders   across her chest.

She lives where tenderness follows
the bruising word   where tell-tale wounds leave
an indelible print.

Sleeps where night is mercenary—
regrets and remorse
their double henchmen.

Odd, how in the dark, regrets find refuge—
come daylight they trail her in shadow steps.

Should her heart open its trap door
tap like a child in the play-penned hour
she will answer—

If only I could, I would…

her refrain grazing
her slumbering heart.

Buoy

Dark steering of love along the curve
and surge

his barbed tongue on the salt of her skin   her red cone
heart tipping like a buoy in the breach of water

warm-blooded float on the open sea
bobs so lightly he can cup it in his hand

tilt it to the current of his choosing
swift and deep.

How to secure a heart
with a knotted rope
of unintended promise?

She gauges the distance
she thought palpable

her hips under his

wave of breath
that follows

now compressed to
dead weight and
a crooked line of air.

Self-Debate on Missed Opportunity

"Missed opportunity, it's all conjecture," said the first of two
characters in my Platonic debate. "Won't profit anyone to mourn it
for long," the man of commerce continued,
his fluorescent market shares bloodless on stark white flow
charts. "I should think we are all prone to error," the second,
a logician, replied.

After spinning this three-wheeler wisdom round
like a scratchy 45 record
after absolving these inflicting characters of any obligation,
I couldn't bar those hypothetical conditionals—
avert their dam flood in my brain.

I should set up a language tribunal
and prohibit "would haves," "could haves," and "should have
been"
once and for all.
They blur the present and renege on the past.

Reeling out the old casualty list
like some war veteran in a musty townhall reunion
Misreading and misunderstanding our pidgin
though we think ourselves adept at well-placed innuendo.

It's as if we said, "Let's deliberately toss a coin—you and I."
See, it flipped on its head and fell down some bottomless grate
So much for possibility
So much for missed opportunity
"Isn't that just like love," we sighed.
always beyond our tentative reach."

A Stay at the Hospital

At night the hallway light casts interrogating searches through the room, panning the plaster walls, zooming in on the fugitive faces of patients. My four-wheel bed rises and falls with the press of a lever. I cling to its metal rails.

A nurse towers over me in a Gulag dream, her bulldog shoulders leaning back, her flashlight blinding my eyes.

"May I have some water, please?" I ask, timid as a schoolgirl.

The wall of my womb has been sliced. My abdomen, numb and gaseous, swells around the wound. Rubenesque in shape, I am a scarred woman whose medical history reads: *nulliparous* (never gave birth).

Fluid waste drips into gift bags. Tied to a plastic tube through a vein, I form a symbiotic bond with a bag of sugar and saltwater. When we do part, I am relieved, waving goodbye as an orderly in loosely fastened turquoise pants leads the two-wheeled stick figure down the corridor.

***

Acts of kindness come sailing into the room too. Family and friends arrive with pots of flowers and boxes of candy, their idle hands and feet steering this way and that. Healthy—not knowing what to do—visitors from the outside are naturally at odds with the place.

Across my bed lies a black woman named Cecelia. Cecelia belongs to a Pentecostal Church. Every day, women come dressed in flowered skirts, white polyester shirts and sunbonnets, surprisingly fresh during that humid week of July. They address her as "Sister," stay with her and pray in a cult around her bed, forming a halo, a ring of love in that antiseptic space for the ill.

Cecilia has a son. Twenty-one years old, she tells me any number of times.

I never see him.

On the last night we are interned at North York's former Branson Hospital, the search light fires across the floor. I hear Cecilia chant repeatedly, "Jesus loves me," clicking her tongue against the roof of her mouth.

In time, I chant in unison with Cecilia. What harm can there be in that? I hold no Bible in my hand. It is easy enough to imitate her Christian devotion.

***

But in her voice I hear the weight of disappointment, and from the dark corners of the room, I sense a vacancy in the absence of sons...a forfeiture of the heart that can leave you a little pale, at the very least, less proud in the way you hold your back, less able to surrender to an occasional wave of irrepressible hope.

For Cecelia, the most blessed son loves unconditionally...I lie in bed and wonder if in her affirmation of his name, she might drink from his cup through the night's passing.

Unnamed

Why is it I most trust a voice
with chinks of loss
that gentle still confesses
love?

Motherhood

In the age before digital calendars
my sister timetabled her daughters' spare hours
each week on the magic-marker colored grid
displayed on her fridge:
swimming lessons, dance lessons, piano lessons.
Because time could hang heavy as a delinquent rope
she packed the burlap bag of a day
sealing out idleness and stray chance
with a knot.

I Linger on Sundays

I linger on Sundays
I am lulled by Sundays
and rest my head
Moving about I do little
and am seemingly content

Comfortable and old boot-worn
I walk in my habits and rest in my frame
For this weekly-earned right
I carry no shame, less so regret

I am motherless and have no children
about whom I should fret

Only myself to answer to
having leisurely read every bulletin, every caper

my faith in a Sunday God reduced to a wager

I tap on the pane
to measure cold's limit
and lightly consider
a neighborly visit

An hour longer
seems to be the most fitting
Only this holds my interest—
to remain silent and sitting

in an armchair deep-set
on this winter's day
when Sunday sits down
and has its say.

Straight Back Chair

from a photograph by Wright Morris, Nebraska, 1947

wall in colorless grey
across the dented floor   tiles in a hexagon pattern
map of lost footprints

framing the shot   a straight back chair
seat chipped down the middle—small tectonic
plate of earth broken

but for the looped carving on its wood panel
the chair is lean   its lines simple

its temperament—if that can be said about a chair—
obstinate

knob on the old farm door is smooth, round
decades earlier, his wife entered in her bib apron,

motioned in mild admonition
that dinner was set on the table

If he had stayed there, sitting on the straight back chair
in fading light and shadow
his backbone poking through the spindles
could he foresee the next crop of corn   wage a deal with God
for a full reaping of grain   smooth his palms against the flatland
in a benediction

for plain-clothed farmers
who bore down
on chairs like these?

What Is Easily Abandoned

—Dauphin in the Desert, 1974, oil on linen by John Salt

stripped tires   rust on a body
long exposed to desert sun
windowpanes dusted in sand

easy to abandon this economic car
of the late 1950s   said to have sped around corners
with the handiness of roller-skates

what else can we discard:
grocery list in a coat pocket, school notes in shorthand
pills past expiry, liquid lipstick run dry

old phone books with names we can't recall
paper calendars thick with appointments we met
minutiae to mark the day

but what of things we outgrow or hold in passing:

furtive secrets of girlhood
promises of the faithful   the intimate—
how tangential that line between us

stem of spring in a backyard garden
impression of beauty in the color of water
eyes of the newborn turning to light

all this unredeemable by cash, points,
or coupon   revealed in the flash
of a speeding train   fog of dream

to the heart that squanders

Jumping Rope

from a once-lost photograph by David Attie entitled "Jump Rope" Brooklyn, New York, 1958

airborne, their lithe bodies diagonal, knees bent on equal plane
girls in striped shirts and summer pants
emboldened by the imagining of flight

one, older and a head taller, stretches her arms
in fleeting independence
(the other's half-figure mimicked on the glass window)

in the background dulled by a mist
Manhattan's skyline replicated in pallid grey

along the waterfront
bulky-headed cars move in succession on the brick road

on the sidelines
back against a bare store front, hands held behind her
a younger pony-tailed girl with a ribbon in her hair watches
confined by a dress with a feminine hoop

shadows, slender and attenuated, stain the patched-up pavement

yet at the center of action—a trick of the eye—
no line of string or braided loop to pass under
to jump through

only two child acrobats defying
the circumference of their girlhood

Letter for Emily D

Convention saw a pallid shell,
and not her myriad color—

Mute to the lyric form she fused
with elemental power.

How she gleaned ripe the natural world,
her open heart, a grail—

And steered ethereal her verse,
its earthly light unveiled.

Poet as Magician

If I were a true poet, I would shape meter
out of a wave of sound   Hone

my primitive craft on a tree's birch scroll
lying low on a twig till the sap rises

Align the bones of words hip-to-hip
fingertips tracing the walls of pages

Dip oars of light on images concealed
conjuring from their imprint
a prism of verse

Seasonal Septet—Lost: Winter Dream Poem

Soft beam of light through the arch
of December's door

from a peerless window

vault of sky breaks open
as snowflakes descend
in sestinas

I fix pattern to memory
pierce rhyme on the roof of my mouth

when a whirl of wind
dissolves into mist

this small inheritance of words

Morning Call

Sweet clamor of sparrows—trill of flutes
banish a dream from my pillowed head.

Bluebirds call on branch balconies,
vie against the morning shuttle
in tender, high-crested
proclamations.

Do they grow weary of their mating song?
Answer only to perfect pitch?
Are we ever as full-hearted in that breath of time?

Ladies-in-Waiting

yellow band of long-limbed tulips
   attend the chamber of the sun

Short Ode to Summer

Under a taunting sun
summer days run long
sag low from the weight of peaches
cluster of figs ready to prune
in my neighbor's garden.

If I could thumbtack the length and width
of her days to a cork-board wall
I'd suppress time
quell its appetite for the offspring of trees
and the cold, imperceptible stillness
of winter's watch.

Discovery

along the bike path by Lake Champlain

Ring of children
study a chrysomelid the color of clay
with the wings of a copper sun. Kneeling

low, they hold their breath
and watch the world teeter.

Dorm Residents

Brock University, Labor Day, 1996

Midday sun squats
bare-bottomed
across a football field.

Bronze-summered men
climb primeval fences
for red tank-topped Helens,
escapees from dull Spartan rooms

as streams of water shoot
love darts between them.

School Announcement

echoing across long corridors
intercom voices crack in static
indistinguishable as the hems of coats
peeking out of high school lockers

through classroom windows
Autumn sears in gold and red

tethered to their seats, backpacks in tow
students gear into first-rate jockeys at the call
bracing at the starting gate
lunging forward on the bell

Malcontent

Prefix comes from the French
meaning: bad, sick, imbalanced

Sadness like a toll charge

stamps out joy
to some unforeseeable date

when you can again claim it
like the middle name you buried
and then unearthed

Israel, 1949

Now and then
my mother and father called out to one another
from under their tattered canopy

in the musical limber counterpoint
of their Hebrew names:

Shoshana
stem and blush of a rose

Ya'akov
seed of masculine certainty

an endearment
sweet as fruit—
mevasseret

planted along the rift
of valleys between them

culled in the land
of embattled love.

Poem for the Music Biz

There are men you meet in your minstrel days
(demo and head shot in hand)—
middlemen who ride success with the grenade
fanfare of a short summer storm.

Knock on their skyscraper doors,
follow their pin ball eyes, their hall-of-fame phrases

while they toss truth like confetti over their shoulders,
break the skin   mince the root of your song
with the heel of their knives.

Your voice sings like a stray-wood thrush,
its melodies barred behind cages.

(I recall names: *Norman, Abe, Bud,* but their faces fade
like ink dye on my thumb)

A year later, maybe more, tap on the same doors
to greet new names engraved on brush gold plastic

body doubles will sit before you—metered men and women
spitting out coins from the slit of their mouths.

Fear of Science

Gene pools interned,
mutations stamped alien.

Chromosomes perfected
along posterity's belt.

Our species replenished
flawless, unblemished.

Long ago Abraham offered his male child—
kindling of wood, blade sharpened
under a patriarchal sun.

Fearless now, Gods of science
climb twisted ladders of DNA;
measure time on molecular clocks;
transcribe the blueprint of our genes;

embed in the womb
mother lodes of gold.

What shape will take
if diversity makes no dent
and we choose, instead,
to invent
our own waking form?

Dirge

in memory of Dorothy K

Standing on cold wet ground,
the wind whipped our bare ankles, our coats, our faces
till we winced from the offense.
Huddled together, we kept safe distance from the site,
our grief unmasked.

The diggers were there first, odd men out
dressed in their workingmen's pants and open-necked collars,
their Dickensian faces, ruddy, grimly removed,
reduced to hands, pairs of hands hoisting and yanking ropes
once the trembling coda "to my mother who gave me life"
was flung down into the chapel of the open earth.

Our silence was born of incongruence more than fear
You cannot understand death in an amphitheater of gravestones
For a moment only, we were schoolchildren
wondering at a treasure chest,
stung by the rectangular casket that would house its resident—
sympathy words—"laid to rest" dangling before us.

Soil frozen from the night's cold
we were ushered away—
spared from the lowering of the wooden frame
as it settled into that sight unseen—
saved from the shoveling of dirt
to cover the face of death.

What remains is the lingering absence of
We resurrect memory in our media hearts
from the undeveloped retina images
to the audible tinkering of recorded voice.

Who will safeguard our secrets if not the dead?
They alone can be our captive listeners.

Trinity

In memory of my maternal grandmother, Dwora Handelsman
October 1942

Seven decades pass
before molten memory rises
to skin of earth.

My mother calls forth a trinity:

—that it was noon hour
when she last saw her mother

—that she ran as her mother pled
through rapeseed meadows
fields coveted by the sun
until darkness fell

—that she found a slit of shelter
and from an attic window
elbows pinned against the sill
watched for her mother's
resurrection.

Before, noon marked the hour of conformity
mesh wire fence and a schoolyard bell
air-tight meals and undisclosed wages
working day divided in half.

Now, midday wears
a magisterial robe.

She rules
in absentia.

Her pendulum
a slender rod
suspends

from grandmother
          to mother
                    to daughter

the premonitory promise
of life.

Isaac Bashevis Singer and Shoes

Photo by Chuck Fishman of Isaac Bashevis Singer reading
fan mail in his NYC living room after being named the recipient
of the Nobel Prize for Literature

Child of Krochmalna Street
its migrating peddlars, page-worn scholars,
droshkies on cobblestones echoing a vanquished past

Descendant of rabbis on a wonder quest
for living ghosts and dybbuks
who haunt the dispossessed

Singer—seed of story in his blood—
who escaped to the city of the harbor and there wrote:
Family Moskat, Shosha, The Magician of Lublin
in his *mamaloshen*—sits

dressed in Sabbath suit and tie
his circumspect head held low as he
leafs through letters from admiring readers
shoes laid out side-by-side—how tidy and contained the room

while in his mystical towns lived seducers and sages
fools and dreamers and those who sharpened their wits
against stone walls   all prey
for the hungry jaws of war

Ode to Aging and its Formidable Force

out of the fracture of living we extract
wisdom—diamond crystal in the rock

while coveted memory recedes
in fleeting shutter speed

we steal glimpses of who we once were
dream in miniature of who we might still be

though age advances
pressing ever forward
in irreversible retreat

Birthright

From all four corners
you can hear
the stiletto cry of voices
delivered from out of the certainty of the womb
Their demand to be recognized
for all things

for the bone of equality
for the blood and water of love.

About the Author

Carol Lipszyc's book of short stories on children and adolescents in the Holocaust, *The Saviour Shoes and Other Stories,* (2014) and her book of poetry, *Singing Me Home,* (2010) were published by Inanna. Her edited anthology of eighty poems on plural facets of the heart, *The Heart Is Improvisational,* was published by Guernica Editions (2017). Integrating chants and narrative for ESL Literacy students, she authored and performed on *People Express* for Oxford University Press. Retired Associate Professor in the English Department at SUNY Plattsburgh, Carol, who holds a doctorate in Education, has contributed arts-based scholarship to international journals. Website: (www.carollipszyc.com).

www.ingramcontent.com/pod-product-compliance
Lightning Source LLC
Chambersburg PA
CBHW031154090426
42738CB00008B/1326